TRIUMPH
BOOKS

Soccer Stars

Content packaged by Mojo Media, Inc.
Editor: Joe Funk
Creative Director: Jason Hinman

This book is available in quantity at special discounts for your group or organization.
For further information, contact:

Triumph Books
542 South Dearborn Street
Suite 750
Chicago, IL 60605
Phone: (312) 939-3330
Fax: (312) 663-3557

Printed in the United States of America
ISBN: 978-1-60078-098-1

Contents

David Beckham

Hometown: London, England
Club: Los Angeles Galaxy

The biggest international superstar in sports today is undoubtedly David Beckham. Coming from humble roots as a fan in London to becoming the face of his sport has been a long journey for Becks, but it's a destiny he has embraced with open arms.

The stunning midfielder was known for his booming and curving free kicks from his teen years, and quickly moved up to the Manchester United reserves to go along with occasional first team appearances. He would also earn notice with the England U-21 side which saw David become one of the most recognized up-and-comers in the soccer world.

His control of the game quickly made him a fixture in the Manchester United lineup, and by age 21 he had secured his place as a star of the team. He also became a regular with the senior national team, culminating in his nomination to the squad that competed in the 1998 World Cup.

Since, Beckham has been at the top of the soccer world and has become an international superstar. He has twice more played in the World Cup for England and has remained a regular on the squad even after leaving old club Real Madrid for the LA Galaxy, making him the first MLS player to play for England. Although he is no longer the captain of the international team, Becks has no intentions of leaving international play.

Since signing with LA, Beckham has exposed himself to an all-new audience in the United States. Even though he has reached his 30s and struggled with injuries David has shown no signs of slowing down and remains the most popular soccer player in the world.

Fast Stat:

6

Years that Beckham was captain of the English national team

Ht: 6' 0" • **Wt:** 165 • **DOB:** 5/2/75

Position: Midfield

2007-2008 salary:
$50 million (actual figure not disclosed)

Career goals/international caps:
76 club goals/97 caps

Personal homepage:
http://www.davidbeckham.com/

Did you know?: David and his wife Victoria have three sons.

As a kid: David, his parents, and two sisters were huge Manchester United fans, often travelling from London to Manchester to see them play.

Favorite foods: David enjoys eating Italian and Chinese food, but also loves English staple fish and chips.

Hobbies: David enjoys other sports, especially boxing and rugby. He says he would have liked to play professional cricket had he not become a soccer player.

Favorite music: Pop music, dance/house music, his wife Victoria and Pavarotti

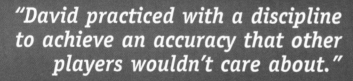

"David practiced with a discipline to achieve an accuracy that other players wouldn't care about."

– Manchester United manager Sir Alex Ferguson

Kaka

Hometown: Brasilia, Brazil
Club: AC Milan

A member of the latest generation of South American players to find success in Europe, electrifying midfielder Kaka has enjoyed success after success in his career.

Coming from a stable, middle-class family in Brazil, Kaka and his brother were gifted from a young age. After attending a local academy at age eight, Kaka signed his first pro contract at age 13. His rise was swift, and within seven years he had been named to the 2002 World Cup squad for Brazil.

His time on that team would be frustrating, however, as Kaka observed more than he played. Only appearing in 18 minutes of action in one game, he returned to his club ready to become a star thanks to his new-found drive to be one of the best.

A star for AC Milan, Kaka is one of only a handful of young Brazilians enjoying immediate success in Europe, a role that is becoming progressively more difficult to attain. Returning to the World Cup in 2006, Kaka started the tournament off with a bang, scoring his team's only goal in their opening game win over Croatia. Unfortunately, the tournament went downhill from there – Kaka did not score again and Brazil was knocked out in the quarterfinals.

A man of deep religious conviction, Kaka spends much of his offseason donating time to help the poor. Since 2006 he has been an ambassador for the United Nations' World Food Program, providing hope for people worldwide.

Fast Stat:

62

Number of career goals in Kaka's first seven professional seasons

Ht: 6' 1" • **Wt:** 180 • **DOB:** 4/22/82

Position: Midfield

2007-2008 salary: $8.4 million

Career goals/international caps: 62 club goals/54 caps

Did you know?: Kaka was nearly paralyzed in a swimming accident when he was 18 but managed to make a full recovery.

As a kid: Kaka enjoyed playing soccer as a kid in the streets and on the beach, always teamed up with his brother.

Fun tidbit: Kaka's brother, Rodrigo, plays with him at AC Milan.

Hobbies: Kaka enjoys spending time with his wife and family, and playing beach soccer.

Favorite music: Gospel

"Kaka has the potential to be the World Cup's most valuable player."

–Brazilian teammate Juninho

Ronaldo

Hometown: Rio de Janeiro, Brazil
Club: AC Milan

One of the most electrifying players in the world for the last 15 years, Ronaldo is a record-breaking superstar. The only Brazilian to score more than Pele for the national team, Ronaldo is a Brazilian hero and international superstar who came from poor, humble roots to get where he is today.

Starting his career after signing his first professional deal at age 13, Ronaldo moved to Europe for a huge transfer fee while he was still a teen. He would also enjoy his first international successes as a teen, notably being named to the 1994 Brazilian World Cup squad. Although he did not appear in any of the games, the 17-year old garnered valuable experience.

He has been a fixture of the national team ever since. He took a bronze medal from the 1996 Olympics and has appeared in the 1998, 2002 and 2006 World Cups. Often playing through injury, the star has broken every World Cup scoring record possible, and is the leading scorer in the history of the competition. Even though the 2006 tournament may have been his last large international appearance, Ronaldo was able to go out with a bang, scoring three goals before Brazil bowed out in the quarterfinals.

A fixture for some of the biggest European club teams, Ronaldo currently plies his craft for AC Milan. Still possessing the two-footed attack that made him famous, Ronaldo remains one of the best in the world.

"In Brazil every kid starts playing street football very early. It's in our blood."

—Ronaldo on his start in the game

Fast Stat:

3

World Player of the Year awards Ronaldo has earned. Only one other player has earned as many.

Ht: 6' 0" • **Wt:** 180 • **DOB:** 9/22/76

Position: Striker

2007-2008 salary: $5.6 million

Career goals/international caps: 227 club goals/97 caps

Personal homepage: http://www.r9ronaldo.com/

Did you know?: Ronaldo is the leading scorer in World Cup history.

As a kid: Ronaldo loved running around outside, on beaches or in fields.

Favorite foods: Pork and beef carnitas

Hobbies: Ronaldo loves going on vacation, especially to visit America. When he isn't playing soccer competitively, he enjoys playing goalie.

Favorite music: Samba and any dance/pop music

Michael Owen

Hometown: Chester, England
Club: Newcastle United

Fourth on England's all-time goal scorer's list, Michael Owen is an English national treasure whose stock has been steadily rising worldwide thanks to new endorsements and appearances.

Signed by Liverpool at just the age of 13, Owen was known for excellence in soccer as well as in the classroom, earning high grades all around while rapidly rising through Liverpool's academy. A star from his teen years on, Owen is still in his 20s, but has nearly a decade of top-flight soccer under his belt with some of the world's highest profile teams.

Playing for gritty Liverpool teams and currently with Newcastle United, Owen is known for his goal-scoring touch and pace-setting play, attributes that have made him a fan-favorite. Although a tough trip on European soil with Real Madrid and subsequent injuries after transferring to Newcastle seemed to slow his play, Owen was still the first choice striker for the English team at the 2006 World Cup.

Although he suffered an injury at the tournament that would keep him out of action for several months, Owen has recently returned to form, helping to guide a resurgent Newcastle squad. Michael is married and has three children, and commutes to Newcastle daily via helicopter.

"For me there's nothing better than putting the white shirt on for England and playing for England. I'd get worried if I wasn't like that."

– Michael Owen on playing for England

Fast Stat:

19

Michael's age when he made his international debut for England, making him the youngest member of the national team since the 1800s

Ht: 5' 8" • **Wt:** 150 • **DOB:** 12/14/79

Position: Striker

2007-2008 salary: $10.8 million

Career goals/international Caps: 138 Club, 41 International/85 caps

Personal homepage: www.michaelowen.com

Did you know?: Michael writes a guest newspaper column for the *London Times* during the offseason or when he cannot play.

As a kid: Michael was very intelligent as a kid, earning high marks in school. His soccer talent was evident from a young age. He was known for his flair and for being a secret weapon due to his small stature.

Fun tidbit: Michael was once training to become a helicopter pilot, but his contract prevented him from actually obtaining the license.

Hobbies: Michael enjoys collecting cars and raising horses with his family as well as playing golf.

Favorite music: Lightning Seeds

Ronaldinho

Hometown: Porto Alegre, Brazil
Club: FC Barcelona

"Every day I wake up with a new dream which I try to make come true."

– Ronaldinho on his daily motivations

A two-time World Player of the Year, Ronaldinho is arguably the most popular soccer player in the world, given his immense European and South American followings. Generating more marketing revenue than even David Beckham, Ronaldinho is so popular he even has a comic book based on him. Rising from the millions of Brazilian children playing beach soccer and futsal in his home country, Ronaldinho's talents were evident from a young age. During a youth league game, he completed an impressive feat by scoring every one of his team's goals in a 23-0 win. Already a small media sensation for his abilities by age eight, he would not be missed by national team coaches. Ronaldinho first competed at the under-15 level for his homeland in 1995, several years after turning professional with a local squad. Already employing some of the stepovers, pace, and ball control that would become hallmarks of his professional career, Ronaldinho rose quickly through the ranks.

It would take a move to Europe to solidify Ronaldinho's place as an elite athlete. He played in France starting in 2001 but it was not until after the 2002 World Cup that he attracted more attention. Signing with Barcelona in 2003, the stunning player has become a mainstay with the team. He has earned both of his FIFA Player of the Year awards with the club, leading them to domestic and Champion's League crowns to go along with his personal success.

Recently, Ronaldinho became a citizen of Spain and he now holds dual citizenship for Spain as well as his homeland of Brazil.

Fast Stat:

23

Goals scored by Ronaldinho in a 23-0 youth team win

Ht: 5' 11" • **Wt:** 175 • **DOB:** 3/21/80

Position: Attacking Midfielder

2007-2008 Salary: $11.4 million

Career Goals/International Caps:
116 club/75 caps (31 goals)

Personal Homepage:
http://www.ronaldinhogaucho.com/

Did you know?: The nickname Ronaldinho literally means "little Ronaldo".

As a kid: Ronaldinho was seemingly born with a ball between his feet. He loved spending time at the beach, playing beach games including volleyball and soccer.

Favorite foods: Ronaldinho loves steak and beans — but has a special place in his heart for when it is made by his mother.

Hobbies: Ronaldinho loves playing video games (he's a FIFA Soccer coverboy) and spending time with his family.

Favorite music: Samba music

Cristiano Ronaldo

Hometown: Madeira, Portugal
Club: Manchester United

Discovered by Manchester United manager Sir Alex Ferguson after a pre-season exhibition match, Cristiano Ronaldo was one of Portugal's best-kept secrets throughout his youth years. Like most top-level professional players, Ronaldo became a solid player during his youth years, signing his first professional developmental deal at age 10. Quickly moving through the domestic league, Ronaldo soon found himself in the academy of the country's highest profile team, Sporting Lisbon.

After his performance in an under-17 youth tournament, professional teams throughout Europe began to take notice, although some, such as Liverpool, still thought he was not ready to advance. Although a very raw player coming up, by age 17 the Manchester United players and Ferguson had decided they'd rather play with him than against him.

Known for his intensity and occasional the-atrics and controversy on the field, no critic can doubt Cristiano's effort. Scoring multiple goals in several games during the 2006-2007 season, Cristiano was twice honored as the Premiership's Player of the Month during the season, a feat only three other players have accomplished.

Still scraping the top layers of his talent, at age 22 Cristiano Ronaldo is certain to be a fix-ure in the lineup for both Manchester United and Portugal for years to come. If his perform-ance in the 2006 World Cup is any indication, Cristiano may be on the fast track to becom-ing one of the best players in the world.

Fast Stat:

17

Cristiano's age when Manchester United players convinced Manager Sir Alex Ferguson on a plane ride that they should sign him

Ht: 6' 1" • **Wt:** 180 • **DOB:** 2/5/85

Position: Wing

2007-2008 Salary: $10.2 million

Career Goals/International caps: 38 club goals/48 caps

Did you know?: Cristiano scored two goals in his first senior game for Sporting Lisbon when he was just 16.

As a kid: A notable neighborhood street soccer player, Cristiano has been playing the game since age 3.

Favorite foods Cristiano Ronaldo enjoys any seafood, but mostly Portuguese codfish.

Hobbies: Watching movies, going on vacation, and the first day of soccer after a vacation.

Favorite music: Ronalda, dance music, electronica and techno

o

Fernando Torres

Hometown: Madrid, Spain
Club: Liverpool

"He is going to set the game alight in this division."

– Reading manager Steve Coppell after Torres netted a hat-trick in Carling Cup play

Already one of the top players in the world, Fernando Torres is a superstar on the rise. Signing a youth deal with hometown club Atletico Madrid at the age of 11, Torres is accustomed to success. Stints with Spain's Under-17 and World Cup teams have simply added to an impressive list of accolades that Torres has earned at the age of 23. Discovered after a youth season in which he scored an impressive 55 goals from his striker position, Torres has been deadly in front of the net from his first kicks on.

Torres is known not only for his pace, but for his technical skill. A fast mover with or without the ball, Torres is right-footed but is equally adept at striking or ball handling with either foot. One of the deadliest threats near the goal in European soccer (either in the air or on the ground), Torres will lay low before striking with unfailing accuracy.

With five seasons with Atletico Madrid under his belt, it was a no-brainer that some of Europe's richest clubs would be after him. Eventually, Liverpool would be the lucky squad, paying a club record transfer fee of over $50 million to Atletico for Torres' services. A man who never scores the same goal twice, Torres has quickly acclimated himself to the English game and is poised for even greater success.

Fast Stat:

75

Goals Torres scored over five seasons in Spain, making him one of three men to accomplish the feat

Ht: 6' 1" • **Wt:** 170 • **DOB:** 3/20/84

Position: Striker

2007-2008 Salary: $9.56 million

Career Goals/International caps:
82 club goals/44 caps

Personal Homepage:
www.fernando9torres.com

Did you know?: Liverpool paid a club record transfer fee to sign Torres.

As a kid: Torres enjoyed two main hobbies as young child — playing soccer and throwing things out his parents' window. He played goaltender until he was nine.

Favorite foods: Any pasta.

Hobbies: Away from the field, Fernando enjoys spending time with his girlfriend and reading (mostly books about soccer).

Favorite music: Rock

Thierry Henry

Hometown: Paris, France

Club: FC Barcelona

"Thierry Henry could take a ball in the middle of park and score a goal that no one else in the world could score."

– Former Arsenal manager Arsene Wenger

One of the top strikers in the world for the last several years, Thierry Henry is not only a consistent goal-scorer — he enjoys new challenges as well. A World Cup Champion and an elite scorer, Henry is the definition of the team-oriented superstar.

After growing up up in a tough neighborhood in his native France, Henry signed his first professional contract for AS Monaco at the age of 13. He would stay with the club until 1998, when his three-goal performance in France's World Cup win saw transfer interest increase. After one season with Juventus, Henry would make his way to Arsenal, the club where he would have his greatest success.

The 2001-2002 season would be a special one for the club, as they won both the Premier League and the FA Cup while Henry garnered the first of his four Premier League scoring titles. After an undefeated run the next season, Arsenal would complete their most glorious era with another FA Cup in 2004.

Deadly from one-on-one attacking situations, Henry is known for his spectacular goals and ability to score from anywhere on the field. He is a first-rate, free-kick taker and is the only man in Premier League history to score 20 or more goals in five straight seasons. With his work in England done, 2007 saw Henry back on the Continent, looking for more success with FC Barcelona.

Fast Stat:

174

Goals Henry scored during his eight years with Arsenal

Ht: 6' 2" • **Wt:** 183 • **DOB:** 8/17/77

Position: Striker

2007-2008 Salary: $12.4 million

Career Goals/International caps: 200 club goals/94 caps

Did you know?: Henry led France in scoring when they won the World Cup in1998.

As a kid: Thierry grew up in a rough neighborhood in France but found solace in playing soccer.

Favorite foods: Chicken, rice, and Caribbean food.

Hobbies: Thierry is a political activist for many topics, most specifically his work against racism. He is also an avid NBA fan, and is close friends with San Antonio guard Tony Parker.

Favorite music: Zouk (slow Caribbean music), hip-hop and rap

Steven Gerrard

Hometown: Whiston, England
Club: Liverpool

An inspiring and commanding player, Steven Gerrard may mean more to his team and its fans than any other player in the world. Born and raised near Liverpool, Gerrard has never played for any other squad and is the heart and soul of the current team. Having stated that he has no intentions of ever leaving the club, Gerrard provides a stability in the midfield that no other team can hope to replicate. Even more impressive, he remains among the top midfielders in the world and competes at an internationally high level as well.

Discovered as a school boy when just 8 years old, Gerrard has been a part of the fabric of Liverpool for nearly his entire life. Despite an injury-plagued junior career with the club, he would make his first team debut at just 18 years old in 1998. By the next season, he had quickly established himself as a regular on a club destined for greatness in 2000-2001. Honored as the Young Player of the Year, Gerrard would score 10 goals for a team that would win the FA Cup, League Cup, and UEFA Cup.

Awards and accolades continued to follow for Gerrard, and in 2002 he was named to England's World Cup team. Unfortunately, surgery forced by injuries caused by a late growth spurt prevented Gerrard from competing. He would appear for England in the tournament in 2006, leading the team in scoring with his two goals.

"I'm a fan myself and I'm frustrated just as much as them when we get beat."

— Steven Gerrard on what Liverpool's success means to him

Fast Stat:

23

Goals Gerrard scored from his midfield position in 2005-2006

Ht: 6' 1" • **Wt:** 180 • **DOB:** 5/30/80

Position: Midfield

2007-2008 Salary: $12.75 million

Career Goals/International caps:
44 club goals/59 caps

Personal Homepage:
www.liverpoolfc.tv/team/squad/gerrard

Did you know?: Steven published an autobiography in 2006.

As a kid: Steven suffered from drastic growth spurts, stopping him from playing for long stretches at a time.

Favorite foods: Chicken, rice, and Caribbean food.

Hobbies: Steven enjoys collecting cars and driving them. He also enjoys golfing and playing pool.

Favorite music: Dance

Michael Ballack

Hometown: Goerlitz, Germany

Club: Chelsea

Germany's captain and premier midfielder, Michael Ballack has enjoyed nearly unequaled success in his soccer career. From his youth on, he always had a knack for scoring goals while not compromising his defensive responsibilities, a distinction he carries on today.

After first breaking into the professional ranks, Ballack immediately lit Germany's Bundesliga on fire. His goal scoring rate as a young professional has been nearly unequaled; Not even David Beckham and Ronaldinho could match the young Ballack's totals in their early seasons. Named Player of the Year three times while playing at home, Ballack left Germany in 2006. Currently a top-flight midfielder with Chelsea in England, it has been nothing short of a successful run in club play for Ballack.

It is when wearing his country's colors, however, that Ballack truly shines. His huge goals against the United States and South Korea in the 2002 World Cup helped to key Germany to a runner-up appearance. Although he missed the final, Ballack had certainly turned heads within his national team. Named the captain for the 2006 tournament, Ballack quickly fell into his new role. Named Man of the Match twice during the World Cup, Michael helped the squad to a third place finish.

"It's not enough to just possess talent, you also have to work hard to be able to reach your goals."

— Ballack on the importance of talent

Fast Stat:

13

Number that Ballack has worn for his entire career, at both th[e] club and international levels

Ht: 6' 3" • **Wt:** 175 • **DOB:** 9/26/76

Position: Midfield

2007-2008 Salary: $12.8 million

Career Goals/International caps:
96 club goals/77 caps

Personal Homepage:
www.michael-ballack.com

Did you know?: Michael's learned vocation in secondary school was "Professional Football Player." He earned high marks.

As a kid: Michael earned some spending money by collecting waste paper and old bottles to trade in.

Fun tidbit: Ballack's favorite movie is *The Godfather*.

Hobbies: Away from the field, Ballack is a strong golfer and enjoys spending time with his family.

Favorite music: Pop, R&B and soul

Lionel Messi

Hometown: Rosario, Argentina
Club: FC Barcelona

"I have seen the player who will inherit my place in Argentine football and his name is Messi."

– Argentina soccer legend Diego Maradona

A humble young man off of the soccer field, Lionel Messi is a dynamo on it. A spark plug that some say is worth more to his club than Ronaldinho, Messi is poised to be the face of soccer in the 21st century. Already drawing comparisons to legendary Argentine Diego Maradona, some by Maradona himself, Messi has some large shoes to fill at the tender age of 20.

Messi has been on the radar of the soccer world for several years already. Although he suffers from a growth hormone deficiency that prevents him from growing taller, Messi has always played a big game. Signing with FC Barcelona at the age of 13, Messi would make his debut with the side in 2003. At the age of 17, he would become the youngest player ever to score for the club in league play.

His great passing and seemingly perfect on-field relationship with teammates even spawned competition over Messi on the international level. Offered a chance to jump ship and compete with the Spanish international team, Messi declined, keeping his loyalties with his native Argentina.

A big match player, Messi was named to Argentina's squad for the 2006 World Cup. Although he did not appear in the teams' first game and only came on as a late sub in the second, Messi was able to make a big impression. He would assist on a goal and score another, making him the youngest goalscorer of the tournament. In all, he would appear in four games in the World Cup, turning millions of heads around the world to see the skills of the small Argentine.

Fast Stat:

17

Messi's age when he scored his first goal for Barcelona

Ht: Ht: 5' 6" • **Wt:** 147 • **DOB:** 6/24/87

Position: Midfield/Striker

2007-2008 Salary: not available

Career Goals/International caps:
21 club goals/22 caps

Did you know?: Lionel's middle name is Andres.

As a kid: Lionel moved to Spain when he was just 13 to pursue his dream of playing pro soccer.

Favorite foods: Argentine barbeque.

Hobbies: Lionel enjoys listening to traditional Argentine music and watching soccer on television.

Favorite music: Samba, cumbi, and dance

Wayne Rooney

Hometown: Liverpool, England
Club: Manchester United

Born and raised an Everton fan, young Wayne Rooney has been in the spotlight from a very young age. With a skill and passion for the game noticed by many, it seemed only fitting that Rooney's first professional club would be the one that he grew up following.

As a teen, Rooney found much success with the Everton youth squad that reached the Youth Cup final in 2002, earning him quick promotion to the first team. Against Arsenal later that year, Rooney would become the youngest goal scorer in the Premier League thanks to his first goal, one that prompted the television commentator to exclaim, "Remember the name Wayne Rooney!" Two seasons with Everton's first team and increasing pressure from local fans would cause the talented young Englishman to seek a transfer, and Manchester United was be quick to snap him up.

Despite the increased media blitz surrounding him, Rooney has continued to excel at both the club and international levels. Rooney would become a mainstay for the English squad soon after his transfer to Manchester United, a feat no doubt helped by his impressive performances in the Euro 2004 tournament. Rooney would go on to make the World Cup squad in 2006, but had a disappointing tournament that would end with an unfortunate red card.

Wayne Rooney is one of the brightest young stars in the game today. He plays for the world's biggest soccer club and is already an internationally known star. Although he hasn't yet had major success on the world stage, fans are cautioned to remember the name Wayne Rooney.

Fast Stat:

3

Goals scored by Wayne in his first Manchester United match

Ht: : 5' 10" •**Wt:** 170 • **DOB:** 10/24/85

Position: Midfield/Striker

2007-2008 Salary: $5.5 million

Career Goals/International caps: 56 club goals/38 caps

Personal Homepage: www.waynerooney.com

Did you know?: When Wayne was called up for his first international game, he thought it was for the U-21 team.

As a kid: Wayne is the oldest of three children, and enjoyed spending time with his siblings.

Favorite foods: Spaghetti bolognese

Hobbies: Wayne enjoys playing video games, especially FIFA Soccer.

Favorite music: Eminem, 50 Cent

Frank Lampard

Hometown: London, England
Club: Chelsea

O ne of the world's great under-rated players, Frank Lampard is a stalwart midfielder for Chelsea who in 2005 finished second behind only Ronaldinho for World Player of the Year honors. A player whose rise has been both slow and steady while at the same time spectacular, Lampard is a fixture for both Chelsea and the English national team.

After starting his career in promising fashion with basement dwellers West Ham United, Lampard was signed by Chelsea thanks to a hefty transfer fee in 2001. Bogged down in his first few years with Chelsea, Lampard would become a classic case of a late bloomer. He would seemingly add a new hat each year with Chelsea: playing every match in 2002, becoming a team leader and Player of the Month in 2003, and finally becoming the centerpiece of a championship squad in 2004-2005.

It was this magical season that earned Lampard his major world honors, scoring an astounding 19 goals in Chelsea's Premiership League winning season. Opponents would unanimously come together after games and praise Lampard, who was finally establishing himself as one of the world's top midfielders. Lampard is currently the top scoring midfielder in club history and the top scoring player currently at the club.

Lampard has not been ignored by his country either, making appearances for the national team starting in 1999. He would not become a regular for several years, and missed out on important tournaments such as the 2002 World Cup.

> *When you are playing with world-class individuals, when you are on top of your game it makes it look even better."*
>
> – Lampard on the importance of his teammates

Fast Stat:

13

Goals Frank has scored for England

Ht: 6' 0" • **Wt:** 165 • **DOB:** 6/20/78

Position: Midfield

2007-2008 Salary: $13.1 million

Career Goals/International caps:
89 club goals/56caps

Personal Homepage:
www.franklampard.com

Did you know?: Although signed by West Ham United, Lampard would actually score his first professional goal while on loan to Swansea City.

As a kid: Lampard grew up around the game, as both his father and uncle played and managed at the professional level.

Fun tidbit: Frank currently has an autobiography being published.

Hobbies: Frank grew up with soccer and loved hanging around with his dad's team, West Ham.

Favorite music: Pop, dance

Francesco Totti

Hometown: Rome, Italy
Club: A.S. Roma

Observers would think that 2007's Golden Boot winner as Europe's top goalscorer would be awarded to a player at a high-profile program. A striker at Manchester United, or Real Madrid, or Chelsea would be more likely to earn the award than one from internationally minor A.S. Roma. It is there, however, that Europe's leading scorer Francesco Totti plays, and it is there where he will stay.

A close-knit family with strong values and work ethic, the Tottis were naturally gifted at soccer. After youth stints around the country, Francesco would mature into a strong player for A.S. Roma, his hometown team. Living with his family and enjoying his mother's home cooking has proven to be the right recipe for one of the world's under-appreciated stars.

That's not to say that Totti has been ignored by pundits and fans, most notably being named to Pele's select list of the world's greatest living players, the FIFA 100. Fans throughout Italy, however, have long been aware of Totti's finesse and nose for the ball; he is Roma's all-time leading scorer and is the most-capped player in the club's history.

Internationally, Totti was nearly kept out of the 2006 World Cup due to a broken ankle. Playing with plates and screws holding it together, Totti turned in some key perform-ances in front of a world-wide audience. He would score the decisive goal in the waning moments against Australia, provide a key assist against the Ukraine, and play the entirety of Italy's semifinal win over Germany. He would last over an hour into the final with France, and when the tournament ended in penalty kicks, Totti would be both an interna-tionally known name and a World Champion.

Fast Stat:

1

Teams that Totti has played for in his career

Ht: 5' 11" • **Wt:** 175 • **DOB:** 9/27/76

Position: Midfield/Striker

2007-2008 Salary: $7.8 million

Career Goals/International caps:
151 club goals/58 caps

Personal Homepage:
www.francescototti.com

Did you know?: Totti played in the 2006 World Cup despite having screws in his ankle.

As a kid: Francesco comes from a very close family that was very supportive. They all still lived together until recently

Fun tidbit: Although he never made it as a professional player, Totti says that his brother was the better player growing up.

Hobbies: Francesco owns a soccer school and a motorcycle racing team.

Favorite music: Pop and classical

Robinho

Hometown: Sao Vicente, Brazil
Club: Real Madrid

One of the most skilled players in soccer today, Robson de Souza (also known as Robinho) is a player fast on the rise. Carefully cultivated back home in Brazil and turned loose on Europe in 2005, Robinho is known for his energetic play and unmatched dribbling of the ball. So skilled with the ball that he almost seems to juggle or even pull off the impossible, the sky is the limit for Robinho.

Making his debut at a young age in his home domestic league in Brazil, Robinho quickly showed himself to be among the top players in South America. Quickly outgrowing the arenas of his homeland, young Robinho set his sights high: Real Madrid.

Coming to one of the biggest clubs in the world shed quite the spotlight on the young Brazilian, and he nearly melted under the pressure. Dribbling too much and embroiled in a contract dispute over his transfer with his club from Brazil, Robinho took time to adjust to the European game.

Utilizing his signature pedaling move and his innate ability to control the game when he has the ball, Robinho has made the tough adjustment to European soccer and is now even drawing praise from – and comparison to – Pele, the greatest to ever play the game. Embroiled in a new rivalry with Lionel Messi, Robinho's club future is bright.

His international prospects are equally strong, as Robinho has played with the senior Brazilian soccer squad since 2003. Earning his first World Cup taste in 2006, Robinho would play in every game Brazil played, starting throughout the group stage.

"This lad will bring us a load of pleasure."

– Pele

Roberto Carlos

Hometown: Sao Paulo, Brazil
Club: Fenerbahce

Although his career is still ongoing, there is nothing Roberto Carlos can do now to change his reputation. He is simply one of the best defenders to play the game. Admired by friend and foe alike, Roberto Carlos was a mainstay of Brazil's back end for three World Cups and has been playing top flight soccer for 15 years.

Roberto Carlos notched his most significant run of club success during the near decade he spent at European power Real Madrid. Playing in 512 matches during his time with Madrid, Roberto Carlos was one of the most feared and respected players in the game. He was so entrenched with the club that he even managed to attain his Spanish citizenship, although he still played for Brazil and retained his Brazilian passport.

A household name in international soccer, Roberto Carlos manned the back end for Brazil in the 1998, 2002, and 2006 World Cups. He would score 19 goals in all competitions while wearing a Brazil shirt but would only notch one goal in World Cup play. Fittingly, it would come in the 2002 Cup, helping the Brazilians win the tournament. After playing in every one of his teams' games in 2006, Roberto Carlos announced his retirement from international soccer.

Roberto Carlos may have his best days beyond him as he turns with new focus to the Turkish league, but he still has plenty in the tank. Still a feared defender, Roberto Carlos is doing anything but limping off into the sunset.

"He is a player with an amazing physical talent, who is also very good, and admired by the media and all the other players. He is capable of doing things the others cannot do in terms of his physical condition, and his work rate is exceptional."

– Real Madrid manager Vicente del Bosque

Fast Stat:

3

Goals Roberto Carlos has scored on headers in his career

Ht: 5' 6" • **Wt:** 165 • **DOB:** 4/10/73

Position: Defense

2007-2008 Salary: $9.6 million

Career Goals/International caps:
61 club goals/125 caps

Personal Homepage:
www.robertocarlos03.terra.com.br

Did you know?: Roberto Carlos was named to Pele's list of the greatest living soccer players.

As a kid: Roberto Carlos was a gifted athlete as a kid, and was a prominent player in Sao Paulo youth leagues.

Fun tidbit: Roberto Carlos scored his only World Cup goal against China in 2002.

Hobbies: Like many Brazilian players, Roberto Carlos enjoys beach soccer.

Favorite music: Interestingly, Roberto Carlos enjoys the Latin musician of the same name.

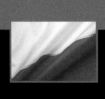

Lukas Podolski

Hometown: Gilwice, Poland
Club: Bayern Munich

L ukas Podolski has had an interesting rise in the soccer world. A Polish-born but distinctly German striker, Podolski made a name for himself thanks to a stirring performance in the 2006 World Cup, oddly enough while his club team sat mired in the second division.

In fact, Podolski was the first German in decades to become a regular on the national team while playing in the second division. Indeed, it is rare to see a talent on any national team that is competitive in the world that plays second division soccer.

Although Podolski had once rescued his Cologne team from the doldrums to the Bundesliga, he would not be around to do it a second time. His performance in Germany's ultimate third-place finish was enough to secure him a transfer, and a big payday, to Bayern Munich, a dominating force in German soccer.

Again, Podolski has shined brightest on an international stage, this time in the Champion's League. Saving some of his best performances for Bayern's key games in the competition, Lukas Podolski is quickly becoming one of the best big-game strikers in the world of soccer. Last year, Podolski became just the third German to ever score 4 goals in an international game, showcasing even more of the potential that he has yet to tap into.

> *"Lukas Podolski is a great performer and we have to let him do what he can."*
>
> – German keeper Jens Lehmann during the 2006 World Cup

Fast Stat:

2

Podolski is one of two Polish-born players on the German national team.

Ht: 5' 11" • **Wt:** 170 • **DOB:** 6/4/85

Position: Striker

2007-2008 Salary: $11.9 million

Career Goals/International caps:
50 club goals/40 caps

Personal Homepage:
www.lukas-podolski.com

Did you know?: Lukas was born in Poland but his family moved to Germany when he was still a toddler.

Fun tidbit: Lukas appears on the cover of FIFA 07 in Germany.

Hobbies: Basketball and music

Favorite music: Lukas will listen to anything, but enjoys dance.

Landon Donovan

Hometown: Ontario, California
Club: Los Angeles Galaxy

Perhaps the biggest star of United States soccer in this generation, Landon Donovan has had a roller-coaster career. From his pedigree with the national team development program to disaster in Europe, to a rebirth back home, the 25-year-old Donovan has already had enough ups and downs for an entire career.

Unlike most players in the United States, Donovan never played college soccer. Going pro at age 18 instead, he figured heavily in the future plans of German squad Bayer Leverkusen. To further season Donovan, they returned him on loan to the San Jose Earthquakes of the MLS to get game experience.

Donovan would become a star in San Jose, quickly proving himself as a dangerous offensive threat. He would star for the U.S. team at the 2000 Olympics in Australia and would become a full member of the national squad later that year.

Landon would figure heavily in the U.S. run in the 2002 World Cup, finding the back of the net twice. With his career on the rise, Bayer decided to recall him from loan in 2005. The Bundesliga, however, would not be kind to Donovan and he would make just seven appearances for the team before being sold to MLS.

He would quickly find himself allocated to the LA Galaxy, and immediately establish himself as a leader on the squad. Now playing with David Beckham and with another World Cup under his belt, fans should be excited to see what Donovan does next.

"Anything with the ball is the best thing you can do, everything else will come to you later, just be with the ball as much as possible."

– Landon's advice to young players

Fast Stat:

34

International goals scored by Donovan, tied for the most all-time for the U.S.

Ht: 5' 8" • **Wt:** 175 • **DOB:** 3/4/82

Position: Midfield/Striker

2007-2008 Salary: $900,000

Career Goals/International caps: 64 club goals/95 caps

Personal Homepage (if any): none

Did you know?: The entire time Donovan played for the San Jose Earthquakes, he was on loan from his German club.

As a kid: Landon played with several U.S. teammates with the national team development program in Bradenton, Florida.

Favorite foods: Crab meat

Hobbies: Landon enjoys outdoor activities and travel.

Favorite music: Landon will listen to anything, especially when it comes to getting pumped up for a game.

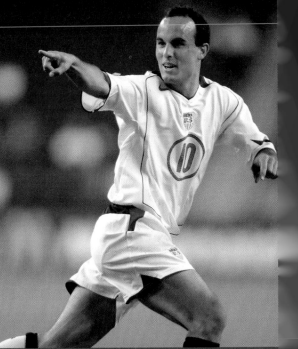

Freddy Adu

Hometown: Tema, Ghana
Club: S.L. Benfica

The youngest person to ever play a major American team sport, Freddy Adu has been blazing trails and turning heads for more than four years and is still only 18. A true example of the American Dream, Adu rose from his roots as a poor Ghanian immigrant to becoming perhaps the most recognizable American soccer player in the world.

Although he just has one senior international appearance, Adu has made waves in several other avenues. Just 14 years old when he signed with D.C. United, Adu proved he was no publicity stunt by scoring 5 goals and appearing in every game United played in.

Freddy may still be maturing physically and mentally, but his skill is undeniable. A regular on sports replay shows with his highlight-reel goals, Adu has quickly become one of the most popular American athletes.

The 2007 U-20 World Cup would be a change of pace for Adu, as he would wear the captain's armband for the first time. Making numerous highlight plays, Freddy was among the best players in the entire tournament. He would return to MLS and Real Salt Lake, but would not stay put for long.

Recently, Freddy was part of a transfer that sees him taking his game to Portugal. Although he one day envisions himself with a big European club, he also states that he would like to represent the USA in three World Cups. If he does, American soccer fans can count on years of highlights to come.

8

Freddy's age when his family moved to America

Ht: 5' 8" • **Wt:** 170 • **DOB:** 6/2/89

Position: Midfield/Striker

2007-2008 Salary: $2 million

Career Goals/International caps:
12 club goals/1 caps

Personal Homepage:
www.freddyadu.com

Did you know?: Freddy was the captain of the United States team at the 2007 U-20 World Cup.

As a kid: Freddy would play soccer barefoot in the streets back home; and in 2003 he became a U.S. citizen.

Favorite foods: Homemade rice

Hobbies: Freddy enjoys golfing with friends and teammates.

Favorite music: Rap

"I just want to get out there and play and have fun. After all, when I'm on the soccer field, that's when I'm at my happiest."

— Freddy on playing in his first MLS game

Jared Borgetti

Hometown: Sinaloa, Mexico
Clube: Cruz Azul

A two-time World Cup participant and arguably the best player in Mexico's illustrious soccer history, Jared Borgetti has enjoyed a stellar career all around the world. Coming full circle, Borgetti has played in his native Mexico, England, and Saudi Arabia before returning to his homeland to close out his career.

Early in his career, Jared shuffled between clubs in Mexico before latching on with Santos Laguna. In his seven seasons with Laguna, he would garner considerable interest from major European clubs but would remain home and win three Primera Division scoring titles in seven years.

In 2005, Borgetti made the move to England, suiting up with Bolton Wanderers. He spent one year with Bolton and played the next year in Saudi Arabia before returning home to Mexico.

While his club career has been a certain success, it has been his international play that has made Borgetti a superstar. He was be among Mexico's top players in both the 2002 and 2006 World Cups, helping to lead his team to impressive finishes. Although he announced his retirement from international play after the 2006 World Cup, recently Jared has said that he would like to return for one last run in the 2010 Cup. If he does, fans can expect the same impassioned and high-scoring performance they have enjoyed from Borgetti for more than a decade. A true Mexican legend, Borgetti can only further solidify his sterling reputation as a star of the international game.

"*Borgetti is a goal scorer. He does very well in getting away from defenders and is able to find the goal at will.*"

– Mexio coach Ricardo Lavolpe

Fast Stat:

7

Clubs Borgetti has played for in his career

Ht: 6' 0" • **Wt:** 175 • **DOB:** 8/14/73

Position: Striker

2007-2008 Salary: $3.1 million

Career Goals/International caps:
243 club goals/87 caps

Did you know?: Although he is Mexican, his ancestors came from Italy.

As a kid: Jared enjoyed playing street soccer and had a lengthy youth career, not making his professional debut until age 21.

Fun tidbit: Jared has scored more career goals than any other player featured in this publication.

Hobbies: Jared enjoys running and reading.

Favorite music: All kinds, but especially traditional Mexican music.

Player Stats

Michael Owen

Season	Club	Games	Goals	Yellow Cards	Red C
2006/07	Newcastle United	3	0	0	
2005/06	Real Madrid	0	0	0	
2005/06	Newcastle United	10	7	0	
2004/05	Real Madrid	20	13	1	
2003/04	Liverpool	29	16	0	
2002/03	Liverpool	32	19	0	
2001/02	Liverpool	25	19	1	
2000/01	Liverpool	20	16	0	
1999/00	Liverpool	22	11	2	
1998/99	Liverpool	30	18	0	
1997/98	Liverpool	36	18	0	
1996/97	Liverpool	2	1		

Ronaldinho

Season	Club	Games	Goals	Yellow Cards	Red
2006/07	FC Barcelona	32	21	8	
2005/06	FC Barcelona	29	17	5	
2004/05	FC Barcelona	35	9	5	
2003/04	FC Barcelona	32	15	9	
2002/03	Paris Saint-Germain	20	8	3	
2001/02	Paris Saint-Germain	19	9	8	
2000	Grêmio	15	8	4	
1999	Grêmio	47	22	4	
1998	Grêmio	48	7	0	

Cristiano Ronaldo

Season	Club	Games	Goals	Yellow Cards	Red
2006/07	Manchester United	31	17	2	
2005/06	Manchester United	24	9	8	
2004/05	Manchester United	25	5	3	
2003/04	Manchester United	15	4	4	
2002/03	Sporting CP	11	3	1	

David Beckham

Season	Club	Games	Goals	Yellow Cards	Red C
2006/07	Real Madrid	12	3	13	
2005/06	Real Madrid	30	3	7	
2004/05	Real Madrid	29	4	10	
2003/04	Real Madrid	32	3	7	
2002/03	Manchester United	27	6	5	
2001/02	Manchester United	23	11	6	
2000/01	Manchester United	29	9	3	
1999/00	Manchester United	30	6	6	
1998/99	Manchester United	35	6	0	
1997/98	Manchester United	37	9	0	
1996/97	Manchester United	36	7	0	
1995/96	Manchester United	33	7	0	
1994/95	Manchester United	4	0	0	
1994/95	Preston North End	5	2	0	
1993/94	Manchester United	0	0	0	
1992/93	Manchester United	0	0	0	

Player Stats

Ronaldo

Season	Club	Games	Goals	Yellow Cards	Red Cards
2006/07	Real Madrid	3	1	1	
2006/07	AC Milan	12	7	1	
2005/06	Real Madrid	21	14	1	
2004/05	Real Madrid	32	21	1	
2003/04	Real Madrid	31	24	6	
2002/03	Real Madrid	30	23	1	
2001/02	Internationale	9	7	0	
2000/01	Internationale	0	0	0	
1999/00	Internationale	5	3	2	
1998/99	Internationale	17	14	0	
1997/98	Internationale	32	25	0	
1996/97	FC Barcelona	37	34	0	
1995/96	PSV Eindhoven	13	12	0	
1994/95	PSV Eindhoven	32	30	0	
1994	Cruzeiro	14	12	0	

Kaka

Season	Club	Games	Goals	Yellow Cards	Red Cards
2006/07	AC Milan	30	8	1	
2005/06	AC Milan	28	14	1	
2004/05	AC Milan	33	7	4	
2003/04	AC Milan	25	10	5	
2003	São Paulo	10	2	2	
2002	São Paulo	20	8	10	
2001	São Paulo	22	12	5	

Fernando Torres

Season	Club	Games	Goals	Yellow Cards	Red Cards
2006/07	Atlético Madrid	34	14	5	
2005/06	Atlético Madrid	36	13	9	
2004/05	Atlético Madrid	38	16	3	
2003/04	Atlético Madrid	35	20	10	
2002/03	Atlético Madrid	28	12	5	
2001/02	Atlético Madrid	26	6	6	
2000/01	Atlético Madrid	1	1	0	

Thierry Henry

Season	Club	Games	Goals	Yellow Cards	Red Cards
2006/07	Arsenal	16	10	1	
2005/06	Arsenal	30	27	2	
2004/05	Arsenal	31	25	2	
2003/04	Arsenal	37	30	3	
2002/03	Arsenal	37	24	8	
2001/02	Arsenal	31	24	4	
2000/01	Arsenal	27	17	4	
1999/00	Arsenal	26	17	6	
1998/99	Monaco	8	1	0	
1998/99	Juventus	12	3	0	
1997/98	Monaco	30	4	0	
1996/97	Monaco	36	9	0	
1995/96	Monaco	18	3	0	
1994/95	Monaco	8	3	0	

Player Stats

Steven Gerrard

Season	Club	Games	Goals	Yellow Cards	Red Cards
2006/07	Liverpool	35	7	1	
2005/06	Liverpool	32	10	3	
2004/05	Liverpool	28	7	3	
2003/04	Liverpool	34	4	2	
2002/03	Liverpool	32	5	4	
2001/02	Liverpool	26	3	5	
2000/01	Liverpool	29	7	4	
1999/00	Liverpool	26	1	5	
1998/99	Liverpool	12	0	0	
1997/98	Liverpool	0	0	0	

Michael Ballack

Season	Club	Games	Goals	Yellow Cards	Red Cards
2006/07	Chelsea	23	5	7	
2005/06	Bayern München	26	14	10	
2004/05	Bayern München	27	13	7	
2003/04	Bayern München	28	7	10	
2002/03	Bayern München	26	10	8	
2001/02	Bayer Leverkusen	29	17	12	
2000/01	Bayer Leverkusen	27	7	11	
1999/00	Bayer Leverkusen	22	3	7	
1998/99	Kaiserslautern	17	4	0	
1997/98	Kaiserslautern	17	8	0	
1997/98	Kaiserslautern	16	0	0	
95/96	Chemnitzer	15	0	0	
96/97	Chemnitzer	34	10	0	

Lionel Messi

Season	Club	Games	Goals	Yellow Cards	Red Cards
2006/07	FC Barcelona	21	10	2	
2005/06	FC Barcelona	11	6	2	
2004/05	FC Barcelona	0	1	0	

Wayne Rooney

Season	Club	Games	Goals	Yellow Cards	Red Cards
2006/07	Manchester United	33	14	5	
2005/06	Manchester United	34	16	8	
2004/05	Everton	0	0	0	
2004/05	Manchester United	24	11	7	
2003/04	Everton	26	9	10	
2002/03	Everton	14	6	6	

Frank Lampard

Season	Club	Games	Goals	Yellow Cards	Red Cards
2006/07	Chelsea	36	11	3	
2005/06	Chelsea	35	16	4	
2004/05	Chelsea	38	13	6	
2003/04	Chelsea	38	10	3	
2002/03	Chelsea	37	6	3	
2001/02	Chelsea	34	5	2	
2000/01	West Ham United	30	7	3	
1999/00	West Ham United	34	7	4	
1998/99	West Ham United	38	5	0	
1997/98	West Ham United	31	4	0	
1996/97	West Ham United	13	0	0	
1995/96	West Ham United	2	0	0	
1995/96	Swansea City	9	1	0	
1994/95	West Ham United	0	0	0	

Player Stats

Francesco Totti

Season	Club	Games	Goals	Yellow Cards	Red
2006/07	Roma	35	26	2	
2005/06	Roma	23	15	3	
2004/05	Roma	29	12	10	
2003/04	Roma	31	20	5	0
2002/03	Roma	23	14	5	0
2001/02	Roma	23	8	6	0
2000/01	Roma	30	13	5	0
1999/00	Roma	27	7	8	
1998/99	Roma	30	12	0	
1997/98	Roma	30	13	0	
1996/97	Roma	26	5	0	
1995/96	Roma	28	2	0	
1994/95	Roma	21	4	0	
1993/94	Roma	8	0	0	
1992/93	Roma	2	0	0	

Robinho

Season	Club	Games	Goals	Yellow Cards	Red
2006/07	Real Madrid	18	6	4	
2005/06	Real Madrid	31	8	5	0
2005	Santos	11	7	2	0
2004	Santos	35	21	5	0
2003	Santos	32	9	7	2
2002	Santos	24	7	4	0

Roberto Carlos

Season	Club	Games	Goals	Yellow Cards	Red
2006/07	Real Madrid	20	3	4	
2005/06	Real Madrid	35	5	6	
2004/05	Real Madrid	33	3	6	
2003/04	Real Madrid	32	5	6	0
2002/03	Real Madrid	37	5	4	
2001/02	Real Madrid	31	4	5	
2000/01	Real Madrid	36	5	7	
1999/00	Real Madrid	35	5	5	
1998/99	Real Madrid	35	5	0	
1997/98	Real Madrid	35	4	0	
1996/97	Real Madrid	37	4	0	0
1995/96	Inter	30	6	0	
1995	Palmeiras	23	3	0	
1994	Palmeiras	24	2	0	
1993	Palmeiras	20	2	0	

Lukas Podolski

Season	Club	Games	Goals	Yellow Cards	Red
2006/07	Bayern München	11	4	1	0
2005/06	1.FC Köln	30	12	9	
2004/05	1.FC Köln	29	24	5	
2003/04	1.FC Köln	18	10	2	0

Player Stats

Landon Donovan

Season	Club	Games	Goals	Yellow Cards	Red
2007	Los Angeles Galaxy	25	8	3	0
2006	Los Angeles Galaxy	24	12	3	0
2005	Los Angeles Galaxy	20	12	3	0
2004/05	Bayer Leverkusen	7	0	0	0
2004	San Jose Earthquakes	22	6	6	0
2003	San Jose Earthquakes	21	12	3	0
2002	San Jose Earthquakes	18	7	3	0
2001	San Jose Earthquakes	17	7	3	0
1999/00	Bayer Leverkusen	20	6	0	0

Freddy Adu

Season	Club	Games	Goals	Yellow Cards	Red
2006	DC United	29	2	0	0
2005	DC United	16	4	4	0
2004	DC United	14	5	4	0
2007	DC United	11	1	0	0

Jared Borgetti

Season	Club	Games	Goals	Yellow Cards	Red
2006/07	Al Ittihad	15	10	0	0
2006/07	Bolton Wanderers	0	0	0	0
2006/07	Cruz Azul	12	4	2	0
2005/06	Bolton Wanderers	19	2	0	0
2004/05	Pachuca CF	13	8	6	0
2004	Dorados	1	8	0	0
2003/04	Santos Laguna	31	22	7	0
2002/03	Santos Laguna	36	27	0	0
2001/02	Santos Laguna	29	23	0	0
2000/01	Santos Laguna	33	41	0	0
1999/00	Santos Laguna	39	22	0	0
1998/99	Santos Laguna	38	19	0	0
1997/98	Santos Laguna	28	14	0	0
1996/97	Santos Laguna	41	20	0	0
1995/96	Atlas	32	8	0	0
1994/95	Atlas	29	13	0	0
1993/94	Atlas	2	0	0	0